# J C Ryle

The man, the minister and the missionary

David Holloway

CHRISTIAN INFLUENCE IN A SECULAR WORLD

This paper was originally given as a lecture in The Christian Institute's Autumn Lecture series on 4 November 2002 at St Stephen's Church, Elswick, Newcastle upon Tyne.

ISBN  1 901086 26 7

Published by The Christian Institute
PO Box 1, Newcastle upon Tyne, NE7 7EF

The Christian Institute is a Company Limited by Guarantee, registered in England as a charity. Company No. 263 4440, Charity No. 100 4774.

# Contents

# Introduction

"One of the most encouraging and hopeful signs I have observed for many a long day in evangelical circles has been a renewed and increasing interest in the writings of Bishop J.C.Ryle.

In his day he was famous, outstanding and beloved as a champion and exponent of the evangelical and reformed faith. For some reason or other, however, his name and his works are not familiar to modern evangelicals. His books are, I believe, all out of print in this country and very difficult to obtain second-hand."

So wrote Dr Martin Lloyd-Jones in 1956 for the reprint of Ryle's book *Holiness* by James Clarke & Co – Lloyd-Jones being a great leader among non-Anglican evangelicals during the 1950s.

Lloyd Jones said that he just happened to "stumble across" Ryle's *Holiness* in the 1930s in a second-hand bookshop. "I shall never forget the satisfaction – spiritual and mental – with which I read it." He, then, summarizes Ryle and his work like this:

"The characteristics of Bishop Ryle's method and style are obvious. He is pre-eminently and always scriptural and expository. He never starts with a theory into which he tries to fit various scriptures. He always starts with the Word and expounds it. It is exposition at its very best and highest. It is always clear and logical and invariably leads to a clear enunciation of doctrine. It is strong and virile and entirely free from the sentimentality that is often described as 'devotional'.

The Bishop had drunk deeply from the wells of the great classical Puritan writers of the seventeenth century. Indeed, it would be but accurate to say that his books are a distillation of true Puritan theology presented in a highly readable and modern form."

Two questions then arise. Why was Ryle not read for many years (and why is he still not read)? During his lifetime his "tracts" – the papers that in the end made up most of his books and were basically printed sermons – were sold literally all around the world and literally in their millions. Why was it that his near contemporary, Bishop Handley Moule of Durham, suffered a different fate? So why was Ryle not read (and why is he still not read)? That is the first question.

The second question is simpler and more easy to answer, why should he be read? In this booklet I will try to lay the groundwork for a straightforward answer to those questions.

# Ryle the Man

Ryle died or (to use the words of the title of one of his famous tracts) he went "home at last", aged 85, on 10 June 1900, just over 100 years ago. He was then buried beside his (third) wife (all three had pre-deceased him) at All Saints', Childwall, on the slope of a hill looking south across the Mersey into Cheshire. Childwall, at the time a rural parish, was where Ryle used to go to be quiet and have time off from the pressures of his busy life as the first Bishop of Liverpool. Liz Holgate, a member of Jesmond Parish Church in Newcastle, was a member of All Saints', Childwall and tells of an elderly member of the congregation who could reminisce about J.C. Ryle - her sister had worked for the bishop.

The Sunday following his death Richard Hobson, a close friend, a clergymen in his diocese and at whose church Ryle and his wife used to worship when free from other engagements, was preaching at the "provisional" cathedral. Hobson spoke of Ryle's greatness in these terms:

> "[he] was great through the abounding grace of God. He was great in
> stature; great in mental power; great in spirituality; great as a preacher and
> expositor of God's most holy Word; great in hospitality; great in winning
> souls to God; great as a writer of Gospel tracts; great as an author of

works which will long live, great as a bishop of the Reformed Evangelical Protestant Church of England of which he was a noble defender, great as the first Bishop of Liverpool. I am bold to say that perhaps few men in the nineteenth century did so much for God, for truth, for righteousness, among the English speaking race and in the world as our late bishop."

Others agreed that he was one of the greatest of the Victorian evangelicals. His successor at Liverpool was F.J. Chevasse. He described him as "that man of granite, with the heart of a child" – the title of a new biography of J.C. Ryle by Eric Russell. Charles Spurgeon, another of the great Victorian evangelicals described Ryle as "the best man in the Church of England."

100 years later many believe that Hobson's was a fair assessment. But what makes a "great man"? J.I. Packer says you need at least achievement and "universality".

In Ryle's case there was the achievement of establishing a brand new diocese (Liverpool had just been split off from Chester when Ryle went there). There was the achievement of his national evangelical leadership. Before going to Liverpool Ryle was a country parson in Suffolk ending up at Stradbroke Parish Church, where he went in 1861. While there he was considered *the* leader of the evangelicals in the Church of England. He led through his preaching and teaching, and travelling considerably. He also led through his other great achievement - his writing. He was a brilliant writer. Unlike many Victorians (and particularly religious writers) he is still readable today. The style is uniquely his own and from a different day to ours. But what he says is crystal clear.

Then in addition to his achievement Ryle was great because of this quality of "universality". Packer says:

"Great men impress us as men not simply raised up for their own day, but as men who are there, raised up by God as we Christians would say, for the benefit and the blessing of generations other than their own."

Yes, Ryle *was* a Victorian. And the Victorians have often had a bad press - sometimes rightly and sometimes wrongly. There was the class system and the social structure which we find offensive today. That affected Ryle in a number of ways. Indeed, the existence of social class was the context for one of the defining moments in Ryle's own life.

Ryle had been born with a silver spoon in his mouth. He was educated at Eton and after Eton at Oxford University, where he excelled both academically and in terms of sport. He was a distinguished classicist. In fact he was one of top three students in his degree year - today, he would have been said to have received a "congratulatory first". He also captained Oxford at cricket - in one university match taking 10 wickets. And he rowed in the university boat race.

Later in life he claimed that his sporting experience gave him leadership gifts:

> "It gave me a power of commanding, managing, organising and directing, seeing through men's capabilities and using every man in the post to which he was best suited, bearing and forbearing, keeping men around me in good temper, which I have found of infinite use on lots of occasions in life, though in very different matters."

However, Oxford was hugely important for Ryle spiritually, especially in his last months at Oxford. He had been made to think about eternity during a period of illness. After he recovered he found himself in a church one Sunday - arriving late! He was just in time for the second Bible reading from Paul's letter to the Ephesians. And the lesson reader, we are told, read clearly and distinctly with a pause between each phrase. This may seem artificial to us, but it had a profound effect on Ryle. The words "for by grace ... are ye saved ... through faith ... and that ... not of yourselves ... it is the gift of God" worked in Ryle's life. They went from his head to his heart. He now understood what the gospel of grace and salvation through faith in Christ alone really meant.

Now, for the context of Ryle's conversion, remember that the year Ryle went up to Oxford was 1834. The University was buzzing with the new Tractarianism – the Anglo-Catholic movement that Newman said started with Keble's assize sermon entitled *National Apostasy* preached in 1833. So Ryle's late arrival at that church and his hearing of the lesson from Ephesians was in the early summer of 1837 – four years later.

As an aside, the Revd J.W. Diggle who served under Ryle in Liverpool before being consecrated Bishop of Carlisle, used to impress upon his ordinands that "Bishop Ryle owed his conversion to the reading of a lesson in church" – i.e., not by a tract or sermon but the simple reading of the Bible. I am afraid you could also say that Ryle was converted by being late to church – that is what gave impact to the lesson – it was the first thing Ryle heard. My wife, being someone who is always early at events, said that if Ryle had regularly got to church in time he might have been converted earlier in life! Ryle was not the best at time-keeping. When later in life he was driven in his carriage to the station to catch the train from the country to London, sometimes people lived in fear and trembling as Ryle was often late and urged the driver to make the horses go faster and faster.

Be all that as it may, Ryle looked back on his conversion in his *Autobiography* that he wrote in 1873, nearly 40 years later, and that reviewed his life up to 1860, "in order," he tells us, "that my children may possess some accurate account of my history of life, after I am dead." So, speaking of his conversion, he says:

> "It may interest my children to know what were the points in religion
> by which my opinions at this period of my life became strongly marked,
> developed and decided, and what were the principles which came out
> into strong, clear and distinct relief when this great change came over

me ... Nothing I can remember to this day appeared to me so clear and distinct as my own sinfulness, Christ's preciousness, the value of the Bible, the absolute necessity of coming out of the world, the need of being born again and the enormous folly of the whole doctrine of baptismal regeneration. All these things ... seemed to flash upon me like a sunbeam in the winter of 1837 and have stuck in my mind from that time down to this. People may account for such a change as they like; my own belief is that ... it was what the Bible calls "conversion" or "regeneration". Before that time I was dead in sins and on the high road to hell, and from that time I have become alive and had a hope of heaven. And nothing to my mind can account for it, but the free sovereign grace of God."

Undoubtedly God had also been working in Ryle's life earlier, not least when he was at Eton.

Giving this paper at St Stephen's, Elswick, Newcastle upon Tyne, I ought to mention that while at Eton Ryle was encouraged to try for the Newcastle Scholarship – a divinity prize established by the Duke of Newcastle in 1829. Candidates had to do a detailed study of the *Thirty-nine Articles* and sit an examination. The top three boys were given a grant of £50 pounds each – which was a lot in those days. Ryle came fourth. He was disappointed, naturally. As at this time he did not show a great interest in Christian things, he probably just wanted the money and the honour. But this piece of study gave him an understanding of Christian doctrine he never had before; and he looked back on the experience as one of the most significant in his life. This is what he wrote later on in his book *Knots Untied*:

"It is a simple fact [that] the beginning of any clear doctrinal views I ever attained myself was reading the Articles for the Newcastle Scholarship and attending a lecture at Christ Church, Oxford, on the Articles by my college tutor. I shall always thank God for what I learnt them. Before that time I really knew nothing systematically of Christianity. I knew not what came first or what last. I had a religion without order in my head. What I found good myself, I commend to others."

So much for Eton and Oxford. He then went back home to his family's estate in Macclesfield which, as the eldest son, he expected to inherit after making his way in law and politics. His father was not too enamoured of the new convert. Ryle describes this time as follows:

"I was training much and learning much in passing through a school of experience which afterwards was very useful to me. I often think now that my chief fault in those days was that I was too much wrapped up in my own daily spiritual conflict and my own daily difficulties. I did not sufficiently aim at works of active usefulness to the souls of others. At the same time it is but fair to say that it would be hard to point out what work there was that I could have done. Teaching, preaching, visitations, evangelization and such like work were out of the question. As long as I lived under my father's roof they would have been strongly objected to, and would have given great offence. It seems to me as if God intended that period of my life to be one of patient learning and not for active doing."

But then something happened. His father's bank crashed. His father became bankrupt losing everything overnight. Here are Ryle's own words:

"My father was a wealthy man. He was a landed proprietor and a banker. I was the eldest son and looked forward to inheriting a large fortune. I was on the point of entering Parliament. I had all things before me until I was twenty-five. But it then pleased God to alter my prospects in life through my father's bankruptcy. We got up one summer's morning with all the world before us as usual and went to bed that evening completely and entirely ruined."

This had a profound effect on Ryle. Writing twenty-five years later he said:

"With all the world before me [I] lost everything and saw the whole future of my life, turned upside down and thrown into confusion. If I hadn't been a Christian at that time, I do not know if I should not have committed suicide. As it was, everybody said how beautifully I behaved, how resigned I was, what an example of contentment I was. Never was there more a complete mistake. God alone knows how the iron entered into my soul; how my whole frame - body, mind and spirit - reeled and was shaken to the foundation under the blow of my father's ruin. I am quite certain it inflicted a wound on my body and mind, of which I feel the effects most heavily at this day and shall feel it if I live to be a hundred. To suppose that people do not feel things because they do not scream and yell and fill the air with their cries is simple nonsense."

## And he felt it *very* badly:

"The plain fact was there was no one of the family whom it touched more than it did me. My father and mother were no longer young and in the downhill of life; my brothers and sisters, of course, never expected to live at Henbury [their family home] and naturally never thought of it as their house after a certain time. I, on the contrary, as the eldest son, twenty-five, with all the world before me, lost everything, and saw the whole future of my life turned upside down and thrown into confusion."

It was not only the sadness and the normal sense of loss that people can understand today. In Victorian society and particularly due to a bank collapse, there was the disgrace, although Ryle had no hand in the collapse. Writing 30 years later Ryle speaks of the "humiliation" of having to leave Henbury – this great estate:

"I do not think that there has ever been a single day in my life for thirty years that I have not remembered the great humiliation of having to leave Henbury. During that thirty-two years I have lived in many houses and been in many positions. I have always tried to make the best of them and to be cheerful in every circumstance, but nothing has made me forget my sudden violent expulsion from Cheshire in 1841 ... Ever since I left Cheshire I have never felt at home, but a sojourner and a dweller in a lodging."

Partly this was because he needed now to earn his living – for the first time ever – which for him meant ordination and working in country parishes, initially for a short time in the Winchester Diocese and then for most of his ministry in the Norwich Diocese – for thirty-nine years in all; and then for the last twenty years of his life in Liverpool as Bishop. All that time he had to live in "tied" houses – that went with the job and that he did not own personally. So this is the man. Packer describes him as:

> "massive (nearly six feet four and strong as a horse, though he confessed to needing much sleep), and his brains, energy, vision, drive, independence, clear head, kind heart, fair mind, salty speech, good sense, contempt for stupidity, firmness of principle and freedom from inhibitions, not to mention an awesome personal aloofness, would have made him a formidable leader and manager in any field. A deep though private conversion experience when he was twenty-one, together with the subsequent traumas of poverty, family shame and the chronic illness and death of two wives over a period of fifteen years, gave him an uncommon measure of authority when he spoke of Christ's power to meet human need."

I have the *Vanity Fair* picture of Ryle dated 26 March 1881 in my study at Eslington House, Jesmond. He does look massive. Actually I was lectured at Oxford by his grandson, the philosopher Gilbert Ryle – sadly someone not known as a Christian, but someone who had his grandfather's gift for simplicity and clarity. He too was massive and seemed to come from the same stock.

Before we leave the subject of Ryle the man, something must be said of his family life. After his short period of work in Hampshire, first in Exbury then in Winchester itself, Ryle found himself in Helmingham in Suffolk and a parish of 300 people. He would be earning there £500 a year – those were the days when there were wide differentials in clergy salaries. This was very attractive to someone like Ryle, with his Victorian and upper class attitudes. It would allow him to marry. Ryle, however, was never sure whether he had done the right thing in leaving his town church in Winchester. He later wrote:

> "Of all the steps I ever took in my life to this day I feel doubts whether the move was right or not. I sometimes think it was want of faith to go, and I ought to have stayed."

But he went and he soon married. He had read the lives of the evangelicals of the 18th century and seen how some of them had had unhappy marriages – for example, John and Charles Wesley and George Whitefield. So he was going to take special care. He had three criteria for the choice of a wife. He wrote:

> "The great thing I always desired to find was a woman who was a Christian, who was a real lady, and who was not a fool. Whether I was successful or not, others must judge better than I can, but I call God to witness these were the three points I always kept steadily in view."

And it was "always" because he married three times. First, at Helmingham, he married Matilda – a woman who clearly fitted all the criteria – on 29 October 1845. Within a year Georgina was born but within a few weeks Matilda was seriously ill and died on 18 June 1847. They were married for under two years. Three years later on 21 February 1850 he married Jessie, another woman who fitted all the criteria. But within sixth months of the marriage, she, too, became ill and hardly recovered over the 10 years of their marriage. Eventually dying on 19 May 1860 she left Ryle with three sons, Reginald, Herbert and Arthur, and another daughter, Isabelle. Within eighteen months of her death, Ryle married, yet again, Henrietta - according to Eric Russell, "a lady of good birth, highly respected, well educated and a woman with a strong personal faith". Ryle married her on 24 October

1861 and they lived happily together for many years, she being a good mother to his children. She was also an accomplished musician and an expert in the new art of photography.

Ryle's marriage to Henrietta coincided with his move from Helmingham to Stradbroke in 1861, one of the richest livings in the Diocese with an income of £1,050 a year.

Just consider, at the very same time (1861) the founders of Jesmond Parish Church, where I come from, lodged with the Ecclesiastical Commissioners (as they were then called) £1000 for the *entire living* of JPC – that is to say it was money to be invested. So only the returns on the money would provide an income for the vicar of Jesmond. And in those days his stipend was considered to be a good one.

So Stradbroke meant a lot of money for Ryle. But Ryle could now marry comfortably (in terms of his own background and expectations) and send one of his sons to Repton and the other two to Eton. It ought to be added, however, that during his lifetime, Ryle was continually still trying to pay off the debts incurred by his father's bankruptcy.

So what was Ryle's home life like? Archdeacon James, one time headmaster of Malvern, and a school friend of Reginald and Herbert, recalled one of his visits to Stradbroke vicarage during the school holidays:

> "Mr Ryle, with his gigantic and stentorian voice, was perhaps rather formidable to a youthful visitor, but he was very kind and hearty, and I soon felt at home ... The atmosphere of the home was, like that of my own home, devotional, daily Bible readings, somewhat lengthy family prayers, and a good deal of religious talk. But it was all quite wholesome and unpretentious, and I don't think any of us were bored, much less cavil at the regime, at any rate at that time."

But life was not at all comfortable for Ryle, as may be gathered. Certainly while at Helmingham life was very hard because of his wife's illness. Listen to this:

"Few can have any idea how much wear and tear and anxiety of mind and body I had to go through for at lest five years before my wife died. I very rarely ever slept out of our own house, in order that I might be in the way if my wife wanted anything. I have frequently in the depth of winter driven distances of twelve, fifteen, twenty or even thirty miles in an open carriage to speak or preach, and then returned home the same distance immediately afterwards, rather than sleep away from my own house. As to holidays, rest and recreation in the year, I have never had any at all; while the whole business of entertaining and amusing the three boys in an evening devolved entirely upon me. In fact the whole state of things was a heavy strain upon me, both in body and mind, and I often wonder how I lived through it."

Ryle was undoubtedly schooled in the school of suffering; and this undoubtedly confirmed his faith in the sovereignty of God. He came to the view that "to feel trouble freely and yet submit to it patiently is what is required of a Christian."

This is how he could write about his experience of the collapse of his father's bank and the consequences:

"I have not the least doubt it was all for the best. If my father's affairs had prospered and I have never been ruined, my life, of course, would have been a very different one. I should have probably gone into Parliament very soon and it is impossible to say what the effect of this might have been upon my soul. I should have formed different connections, and moved in an entirely different circle. I should never have been a clergyman, never have preached, written a tract or book. Perhaps I might have made shipwreck in spiritual things. So I do not mean to say at all, that I wish it to have been different to what it was."

However, he then added these words:

"All I mean to say is that I was deeply wounded by my reverses, suffered deeply under them, and I do not think I have recovered body and mind from the effect of them."

He wrote all that at Stradbroke and *after* he was happily married to a woman who was robust and stayed alive! So much for Ryle the man.

# Ryle the Minister

First, there was his preaching. Unlike Spurgeon, who I read regularly but find difficult, Ryle is simple and clear. Ryle was not only a clear writer because he was a clear thinker, he also studied to be clear. In his early days at Winchester he spoke of his sermons being …

> "… far too florid, and far less simple and direct than I afterwards found valuable. Nevertheless, they were thoroughly evangelical and being well composed and read with a great deal of earnestness and fire. I have no doubt they sounded very fine and effective, but I should not wish to preach them now."

In his book *The Upper Room* there is a paper entitled "Simplicity in Preaching". It was a paper given to clergy much later in St Paul's Cathedral and is still worth reading. It expresses Ryle's mature views. He made five substantial points. First, "have a clear view of the subject upon which you are going to preach." Secondly, "try to use in all your sermons, as far as you can, simple words." Thirdly, "take care to aim at a simple style of composition." Fourthly, "use a direct style." [i.e. using "I" and "you" and not "we"]. Fifthly, "use plenty of anecdotes and illustrations."

So what was Ryle's own preaching really like? He certainly wanted it to be Christ centred:

> "If there is no salvation excepting by Christ we must not be surprised if ministers of the gospel preach much about him. They cannot tell us too much about the name which is above every name. We cannot hear of him too much. We may hear too much about controversy in sermons, we may hear too much of works and duties, of forms and ceremonies, of sacraments and ordinances, but there is one subject which we never hear too much of, we can never hear too much of Christ."

But how did people respond to his preaching? A journalist once attended a service at Helmingham and reported as follows:

> "The sermon was one of the longest we have met with, but the earnestness of the preacher's manner and ever ready flow of ideas, the simple yet forceful language and the wonderfully apt and forceful illustrations made the time pass very pleasantly, and we, who for that time at least had no pudding to be spoiled, were almost sorry when he concluded."

And Ryle usually ended with a note of practical application. For example, in part of his conclusion in *The Best Friend*, which you can read in his book *Practical Religion*, Ryle says this:

> "If Christ is your friend, you have great privileges, and ought to walk worthy of them. Seek every day to have closer communion with him, who is your friend, and to know more of his grace and power. True Christianity is not merely believing a certain set of dry abstract propositions; it is to live in daily personal communication with an actual living person – Jesus the Son of God. 'To me,' said Paul, 'to live is Christ' (Phil.1 :21). Seek every day to glorify your Lord and Saviour in all your ways."

Ryle saw steady but not spectacular growth throughout his ministry. Any lack of response saddened him, but he did not despair. In a sermon he preached in Chester Cathedral in 1878, two years before moving to

Liverpool, he said this:

> "That grand bell in St Paul's Cathedral, London, had struck the hour for
> many years. The roar and din of traffic in the streets have a strange power
> to deaden its sound, and prevent men hearing it. But when the daily work
> is over, and desks are locked and doors are closed, and books are put away,
> and quiet reigns in the city, the case is altered. As the old bell at night
> strikes eleven, and twelve, and one and two and three, thousands hear it
> who never heard it during the day. So I hope it will be with many a one
> in the matter of his soul. Now, in plenitude of health and strength, in the
> hurry and whirl of business, I fear the voice of your conscience is often
> stifled and you cannot hear it. But the day may come when the great bell of
> conscience will make itself heard, whether you like it or not."

But Ryle's services were not just lectures. He was a great lover of
singing. He published collections of hymns. *Spiritual Songs* was his
first collection of hymns for use at cottage meetings. There were then
two more collections, *Hymns for the Church on Earth*, selected for the
use of the sick and lonely, and *The Additional Hymnbook* for general
use. In the Preface to this collection he writes:

> "I strongly hold that holy thoughts often abide for ever in men's memories
> under the form of poetry, which pass away and are forgotten under the
> form of prose."

He also comments on the increasing popularity of hymns in Christian
meetings, saying:

> "I regard with deep satisfaction the growing taste for hymn singing and
> praise, as an essential part of Christian worship. It is the healthiest sign of
> our times ... Nothing is so likely to heal 'our unhappy divisions', and to
> make us of 'one mind' as an increased spirit of praise as well as prayer."

Ryle would like to have thought his ministry was in line with the great
Puritans. He had a great respect for Richard Baxter, the 'Prince of

Puritans' and rector of Kidderminster, famous for his *The Reformed Pastor*. Of him Ryle said this:

> "While others were entangling themselves in politics, and burying their dead amidst the potsherds of earth, Baxter was living a crucified life, and daily preaching the Gospel. I suspect he was the best and wisest pastor that an English parish ever had, and a model that many a modern rector or vicar would do well to follow."

Ryle's general assessment of the Puritans he sought to learn from was as follows:

> "With all their faults, weaknesses and defects, [they] alone kept the lamp of pure evangelical religion burning in the times of the Stuarts; they alone prevented Laud's Popish inclinations carrying England back into the arms of Rome. It was they who fought the battle of religious freedom, of which we are reaping such fruits. It was they who crushed the wretched spirit of inquisitorial persecution which misguided High Churchmen tried to introduce into this land. Let us give them the honour they deserve."

And Ryle was a great believer in visiting. In his paper on *Simplicity in Preaching* he tells of …

> "… a humble country clergyman was once asked whether he studied the fathers [meaning the Early Church Fathers] to which the worthy man replied that he had little opportunity of studying the fathers as they were generally in the fields when he called. But he studied the mothers more because he found them at home and could talk to them. Wittingly or unwittingly, the good man hit the nail right on the head. We must talk to our people when we are out of church if we would understand how to preach to them when they are in church."

So what was Ryle's ministry like in reality – with his major work being done at Stradbroke? A contemporary sums it up like this:

"In parish work he was practical and thorough, taking great interest in the temporal as well as the spiritual welfare of his parishioners. Three services on Sundays, meetings during the week at different places. Well-attended, bright and hearty congregational singing, service plain and forcible, rarely concluded without some words to boys and girls in the congregation. Ryle urged parents to bring young children. Some twenty or thirty years ago (Stradbroke was one of the worst places in the neighbourhood) a respectable person could hardly ride through without being insulted or very likely his hat would be knocked off his head. Now a quieter and more orderly parish is hardly found."

# Ryle the Missionary

You may think that is a strange description. But Ryle was a missionary. He was concerned to see people converted and then built up in the faith – he wanted in today's jargon, not just decisions but disciples – in his terms justification *and* sanctification. Packer speaks of Ryle's agenda and that he …

> "… aimed at four things: the evangelising of English people; the purging of the English national Church; the uniting of English Christians; and the holiness of English believers."

His standpoint was unashamedly evangelical. From the 1850s Ryle became nationally known for his uncompromising evangelical position and his expository preaching, and not only in Norwich diocese. That was through his attendance at meetings in London and preaching in London. But he was especially known for his tracts and then his larger publications. And the major part of this literary work was completed during the period he was at Stradbroke.

"Tracts" were more than brightly coloured leaflets with a few texts. They were serious short papers and were already famous through the Oxford Movement with Newman and Keble and Pusey, who were known as "The Tractarians". Ryle saw the potential. So these tracts were the main vehicle of Ryle's missionary work. He began to adapt his sermons into tracts with suitably striking titles, 'Have you a Priest?' 'Do you want a Friend?' 'Are you Happy?' Before long Ryle's name was widely known both in Britain and throughout the world. Millions of copies of his tracts were produced and then formed and bound into collections called *Home Truths*. Subsequently they formed parts of other works.

His first tract had a tragic origin and was literally 'a tract for the times'. On 9 May 1845 a large crowd had gathered for the official opening of a new suspension bridge in Great Yarmouth. The bridge suddenly collapsed during the ceremony and over a hundred people were thrown into the water and drowned. The disaster shocked the whole country and Ryle took the opportunity to write a pamphlet on the theme of life's uncertainties and God's sure provision of salvation in Christ. Thousands of copies were sold.

Let Ryle summarize his major writings himself. I am going to give an extended quotation from Ryle's own Preface to *Practical Religion* – a collection that first appeared in 1878:

> "The volume now in the reader's hands is intended to be a companion to two other volumes which I have already published, entitled *Knots Untied* and *Old Paths*.
>
> *Knots Untied* consists of a connected series of papers, systematically arranged, about the principal points which form the subject of controversy among Churchmen in the present day. All who take interest in such disputed questions as the nature of the Church, the Ministry, Baptism, Regeneration, the Lord's Supper, the Real Presence, Worship, Confession, and the Sabbath, will find them pretty fully discussed in *Knots Untied*.
>
> *Old Paths* consists of a similar series of papers about those leading doctrines of the gospel, which are generally considered necessary to salvation. The inspiration of Scripture, sin, justification, forgiveness,

repentance, conversion, faith, the work of Christ, and the work of the Holy Spirit, are the principal subjects handled in *Old Paths*.

The present volume contains a series of papers about "practical religion", and treats of the daily duties, dangers, experience, and privileges of all who profess and call themselves true Christians. Read in conjunction with another work I have previously put out, called *Holiness*, I think it will throw some light on what every believer ought to be, to do, and expect.

One common feature will be found in all the three volumes. I avow it frankly at the outset, and will not keep it back for a moment. The standpoint I have tried to occupy, from first to last, is that of an Evangelical Churchman.

I say this deliberately and emphatically ... After 40 years of Bible reading and praying, meditation and theological study, I find myself clinging more tightly than ever to "evangelical" religion, and more than ever satisfied with it. It wears well; it stands the fire. I know no system of religion which is better. In the faith of it I have lived for the third of a century, and in the faith of it I hope to die.

The plain truth is, that I see no other ground to occupy, and find no other rest for the sole of my foot. I lay no claim to infallibility, and desire to be no man's judge. But the longer I live and read, the more I am convinced and persuaded that Evangelical principles are the principles of the Bible, of the Articles and Prayer-book, and of the leading Divines of the reformed Church of England."

But what did Ryle mean by "evangelical" religion? This is what he says in *Knots Untied*. He writes of its "leading features":

"These I consider to be five in number.

a) The first leading feature of Evangelical Religion is the *absolute supremacy it assigns to Holy Scripture*, as the only rule of faith and practice ... Show us anything plainly written in that Book, and, however trying to flesh and blood, we will receive it, believe it, and submit to it. Show us anything, as religion, which is contrary to that Book, and, however specious, plausible, beautiful, and apparently desirable, we will not have it at any price … Here is rock: all else is sand.

b) The second leading feature in Evangelical Religion is *the depth and prominence it assigns to the doctrine of human sinfulness and corruption* … All men … are not only in a miserable, pitiable, and bankrupt condition, but in a state of guilt, imminent danger, and condemnation before God. They are not only at enmity with their Maker and have no title to heaven, but they have no will to serve their Maker, no love to their Maker, and no meetness for Heaven … Hence we protest with all our heart against formalism, sacramentalism, and every species of mere external or vicarious Christianity. We maintain that all such religion is founded on an inadequate view of man's spiritual need. It requires nothing less than the blood of God the Son applied to the conscience, and the grace of God the Holy Ghost entirely renewing the heart … Next to the Bible, as its foundation, it [i.e. evangelical religion] is based on a clear view of original sin.

c) The third leading feature of Evangelical Religion is *the paramount importance it attaches to the work and office of our Lord Jesus Christ*, and to the nature of the salvation which he has wrought out for man … All who believe on Him are, even while they live, completely forgiven and justified from all things – are reckoned completely righteous before God … We hold that an experimental [i.e. experiential] knowledge of Christ crucified and interceding, is the very essence of Christianity, and that in teaching men the Christian religion we can never dwell too much on Christ himself, and can never speak too strongly of the fullness, freeness, presentness, and simplicity of the salvation there is in him for every one that believes … We say that life eternal is to know Christ, believe in Christ, abide in Christ, have daily heart communion with Christ, by simple personal faith, and that everything in religion is useful so far as it helps forward that life of faith, but no further.

d) The fourth leading feature in Evangelical Religion is the *high place which it assigns to the inward work of the Holy Spirit in the heart of man* … We maintain that the things which need most to be pressed on men's attention are those mighty works of the Holy Spirit, inward repentance, inward faith, inward hope, inward hatred of sin, and inward love to God's law … We hold that, as an inward work of the Holy Ghost is a necessary thing to man's salvation, so also it is a thing that must be inwardly felt … there can be no real conversion to God, no new creation in Christ, no new birth of the Spirit, where there is nothing felt and experienced within … We insist that where there is nothing felt within the heart of a man, there is nothing really possessed.

e) The fifth and last leading feature in Evangelical Religion is the importance which it attaches to the outward and visible work of the Holy Ghost in the life of man … The true grace of God is a thing that will always make itself manifest in the conduct, behaviour, tastes, ways, choices and habits of him who has it. It is not a dormant thing … To tell a man he is "born of God," or regenerated, while he is living in carelessness or sin, is a dangerous delusion … Where there is the grace of the Spirit there will always be more or less fruit of the Spirit … where there is nothing seen, there is nothing possessed."

# Conclusion

I have said nothing about Ryle the bishop. That is because Ryle was not perfect. I try to make all the staff at Jesmond Parish Church read one of the original papers in *Knots Untied* (now reprinted in *Warnings to the Churches*) entitled "The Fallibility of Ministers". His argument is that the Bible alone is infallible. Christian leaders can fail and do fail. "The Reformers were honoured instruments in the hand of God for reviving the cause of truth on earth. Yet hardly one of them can be named who did not make some great mistake."

Another of Ryle's books that I reread every year and try to get as many others to read, as I can, is *Christian Leaders of the 18th Century*. Those men were remarkable. But two of them, Ryle reminds us, "abused each other in most shameful language" – he is referring to Wesley and Toplady.

And Ryle made mistakes as a bishop in Liverpool – not doctrinal mistakes but managerial mistakes. It would take another paper to explain. In simple terms Ryle saw more than most the need for biblical truth and the recovery of biblical truth. He was less clear in seeing, or being aware of, the need for leadership skills; for an understanding of the dynamics of large organizations such as the new diocese of

Liverpool; and for strategizing as urban development mushroomed. Ryle could lead remarkably in a small environment using his own personality and personal gifts. But in a large diocese and trying to motivate people indirectly as well as directly was another matter. To be fair on Ryle, many other bishops in the Church of England probably did far worse. The root problem was the problem that is with us now in the Church of England – the Church was getting so comprehensive that it was getting unmanageable, with ritualists and liberals defying the unifying theology of the Articles and the Prayer Book.

But, of course, he did much good work in Liverpool. His significant work, however, undoubtedly came through his writing and most of this was completed at Stradbroke.

Finally, those two questions. First, why was Ryle not read for many years and why is he still not read? And, secondly, and more simply and more easily answered, why should he be read now?

Why was he not read? Answer – too many evangelicals in the Church of England were captured by the 19th century second blessing movement of instant holiness, to which Ryle's *Holiness* was both a protest and an answer; then many middle-of-the-road Anglicans were captured by a liberal theology that surrendered the authority of the Bible to the authority of human reason; and old-fashioned High Churchmen were captured by a Romanizing Anglo-Catholicism that surrendered the authority of the Bible to the authority of the visible church and church tradition. Ryle became a lone voice crying in the wilderness. He was felt to be out of touch. He is still not read for the same reasons. The Bible by too many is no longer held to have supreme authority.

Why should he be read? Because the Bible *is* our supreme authority and Ryle is a brilliant expositor of biblical religion and a brilliant expositor of the Bible itself. If you doubt that, start reading his *Expository Thoughts on the Gospels*.